selected poems

EYES HAVE I THAT SEE

John Julian

PARACLETE POETRY

PARACLETE PRESS
BREWSTER, MASSACHUSETTS

WITH LOVING THANKS TO

a teacher	*a friend and brother poet*	*a friend and editor*
Evelyn L. Schultz	Raymond Roseliep	Jon Sweeney
(1906–1991)	(1917–1983)	(1967–)
"Oh, you must write more!"	"You simply must publish."	who did.

2015 First printing

Eyes Have I That See: Selected Poems

ISBN 978-1-61261-640-7

Library of Congress Cataloging-in-Publication Data

Julian, John, 1932-
[Poems. Selections]
Eyes have I that see : the selected poems of John Julian.
pages cm
Includes index.
ISBN 978-1-61261-640-7 (paperback)
I. Title.
PS3610.U5344A6 2015
811'.6—dc23 201404041904

10 9 8 7 6 5 4 3 2 1

Published by Paraclete Press
Brewster, Massachusetts
www.paracletepress.com

Printed in the United States of America

CONTENTS

THE POEMS

ANIMA CHRISTI

Soul of Christ, O, consecrate me;
Flesh of Christ, emancipate me;
Blood of Christ, intoxicate me;
Water from Christ's side, repair me;
Sufferings of Christ, prepare me;
O good Jesu, deign to spare me;
In thy wounded bosom bear me;
From thy presence never send me;
From the Enemy defend me.
When I come to die, protect me,
And to join thee, Lord, direct me.
With thy blessèd saints upraise me,
That forever I may praise thee. Amen.

THE APPLE TREE

My golden fruit
Lies tarnished now,
The treasures of Hesperides
The toys of children
In a newer world
Which knows no heroes,
Cleaves no violet seas,
And hates the gods.

My leaves
That caught the light
And turned it dancing
Green upon the waters
Curl their death throes
Into permanence
Against the earth;

And I stand naked now,
Ashamed,
And twisting into
Insignificance,
I claw out this injustice,
Crippled now,
Against an orange sky,

Weeping
For a world
Without a Heracles.

CARE

Small shadows of adventure pass behind
My eyes, and little yesterdays concern
The neatness of the ordered, beaten now,
While sparks and shades and fleeting hints that turn
To sometimes marigolds collect and drift
About the edges of today and I
Remember them. And I remember, too,
The fatal endings and black stumps and high
Burned rocks and painful wisps of telltale smoke,
Remaining embers dying on the shore,
Their fading ash between the day and night.
So I take care that I remember
                              ...and no more.

LONG WANDERINGS

One chooses
that is the complication
And looks and weighs
and waits
long wanderings,
essays at balance,
pretensions about both,
But one knows,
and in or out and deep or long,
one chooses.

Suns never rise again
the same,
nor do the waves.

One chooses
and the other roads are gone,
wending
into foothills which
will always be horizon now
and never home—
and rivers pass,
occasioning bridges now
and dams,
not bearing boats.

All that flows or flees or beckons now
is alien,
What stands now is,
and ages.

One chooses
    and finds the dyings
        and the life.

CLOISTER

Can there be still one voice that sings
Of old and near-forgotten things?
Can still some tongue find will to care
For deep and silent wells of prayer
And lives in fameless fasting spent
And cloisters where the hearts are bent
In whispered cycles, lifting days
And nights upon the wheel of praise?

Can still some heart remember now
The trembling power of the vow,
And honor with a mem'ry's grace,
The wonder of a holy place
Where once a simple soul unfurled
Could rise beyond a tepid world
And reach and walk the deeper way?
Or are those foolish things today—

Dull relics of a childish age
Before the scientific mage
Waved potent wands of glass and steel
And trod beneath a modern heel
The dreams and riches of a grace
Which kept alive the human race?
God save us, then, if that be true,
For we are done, and all is through.

DEDALUS

I spoke to him of flying,
and he thirsted
when he heard the sounds
of that high winding country
in the soughing tops of trees,
the bounds of homeland in a glance,
the stepping, deeping edge of sea,
the age-twist of the antique river,
the older sunset and the newer dawn,
the trust of thrust on nature's truth.

He wanted wings
and they were there within my way:
the avid muscle-mold writ large,
the slip-fold of the drum-head pinions,
beyond the function into glory.

We went at once as one—
so he could be a man as well.

I should have known
that he would worship nature
even while I took him
high above his own,
and, not knowing or caring,
for the specificity of splendor.

So he mounted that broad, bright,
    unsaddled back of wind
and dropped the rein and bit,
and ran, ran mad,

perverting wings
and losing manhood
as he died
against the tight and natural
goal of light;

but I, remaining man,
remaining winged,
exploited and enlivened wind
and whipped it to compliance
and was carried at my will.

Thus I could watch
the wing-failed child
fulfill the natural that drove him
in the distant, low and meager
splash of life.

He proved his course of nature,
repudiating will,
and followed close his killer
into the western bath of sea,
setting his glory
because he thought he would be free.

So I go on
and know what no one knows alive,
a votary alone who sees the day
the way Apollo does,
the dark star-wise,
from there—

But always, crucified across
That gray-green-blue of coverlet reality,
I see a flying, dying boy,
wings godding him,
but he unwilling even then
to fight the wind.

If I would have another son,
would there be wings again?
For me
would ever there be wings again?

DOWN WITH MARIGOLDS

If gray could rule
The throbbing summer world
And sweep the golden gleam of marigolds
Beneath its careful mediocrity,
Then we could sleep—
And quite forget about the day
And all the dangers of its worth
And all its costly, bright variety
Which treacherously lies in wait
For sleepy men—
And we could then be comfortable
—and dead.

EYES HAVE I THAT SEE

Eyes have I that see
    behind the eye,
    within the tree
    above the sky,
And lips that sing
    the sound of everything
    I see.
I wonder: do they see as I
    who do not sing?

THE GALLEY-MAN

In chained darkness and
against the pitching hull,
between the bend and reach,
there is a moment when,
above one arching back,
across an arm,
there is
one brusque moment when
along the slant of oar
and through the port,
a patch of sea:
the enemy,
the lover,
all the light I know,
raked high,
green-gray,
the day.

GETHSEMANE, BC

My son, there is no other way.

I walked the grayness of the night
and paced the blooming birth of day,
wreathing casuistic circles,
clouds to hide the pains of truth,
but all those shrouds of delicate theology
dispersed at dawn.

The word refuses to be veiled.

My lovely son, I know that you are limboed
when your eyes are opened on this day:
without redemption or escape.

I pored for double-meaning in the words
within the revelation:
date,
time,
place,
in prefect Hebrew
without the hope of even a syntactic flaw
to be a straw
to cling to.

My son, were there another way,
or but one hint, or one provision,
one canon claused or one permissive rubric,
I could find a hope.
But heart is traitor to my will
and to my fatherhood,

and knowing only truth,
cries only, "Act."

One last sad kindness:
it was not demanded that you know
and will be spared the fear
that tempts to sin
and "No."

But now the lads are washing
and the beast is burdened
    (I did it by myself—
    to find a thing to push today away)
and now the masquerade…

Arise,
my son, arise;
Isaac, arise.

THE GRAIL

In wild unwise Arthurian hands
the painful sea-cup held
against the stars
and mooned the face it was
in sudden silver song
as blind eyes hurtled to the hopeless black
before the Word.

It is what it contains
in all the breathless sanguine terror
of I AM
and this poor blackened womb
refuses and refuses
seas of saving ayes.

Offerimus rings hollow
in the white angelic quest
that grants a bastard son
a bid to glory
in the folded faintness of an old affirmative
as heaven waits to open for a nod.

HE SLEEPS

He rests, who needs no sleep;
The Maker now is made.
He cries, who cannot weep;
The Bearer now is borne.
He lisps, who is the Word;
The Mother still is maid.
He needs, who reigns as Lord;
And Life itself is born.
He sucks, who needs no bread;
The Holder now is held.
He rests, who has no bed;
The Master now is son.
He waits, who knows no hour;
The Unseen is beheld.
He fears, who holds all power;
The Only now is one.

IN CORPORE
(for Ascensiontide)

Go whirling through
your swirling clouds of glory,
and wing your windless way on high.

But turn, sometimes, in glory,
and recall Gethsemane,
the sweat and fleshy press
of Golgotha, and see

I am the world you are—your will,
your body bear the marks of man,
and you are mine,

For you involved me in
that warm eternity of you
and, changeless now, you are of me,
and I, created now, am you.

JUST ONCE MORE

The luminescent twilights of Septembers
I remember,
spiked and exclamated by
the fluting cries of boys in love with day.

But mostly I recall
the sad reluctance to vacate
a day and summer,
and the scuffled, dragging feet
and banged screen doors

with parting calls and promises
and stalling pleas and
ages of compounded ritual
to head off
home and bed.

The sad, reluctant twilight of Septembers
I remember
as I hesitate to die.

LAMENT

On a far lost day,
a sounding seagull's soar
set proud the wide blue waste
and sketched the weak horizon
with whip-bent wings—all pride stiff.

What prey that day,
whirling and willing,
under a silent sun;
what hopes that
now breach knowledge
in the hopeless wash
of tide?

As a fragile skull
of a gray-white gull
moves water ways,
swung and rolled
by the swell
of the earth-girt tides
and the wander of sea and sand.

God save the day,
and the work,
and the love,
and roll my song-skull
through the seas
until he hears it sing
between the waves
and knows death-dying
that I sang
of him.

LONGING

I turned
and stupid staring
saw the sundial fretted
with the scars of shadowed moments
born forever in communion of identity.

And watched the hundred patient moons
each permanent
and old beyond its years.

The world leaned heavy on its staff
and waited
for no star could turn
against the fragment
of the night-gray gull
who hung and soared and tried
to make forever now.

OBLATION

In all that I do,
    You act;
In all that I say,
    You speak;
In all that I wish,
    You will;
In all that I am,
    You are.

THE BEE

The golden-hungered past,
the stones on which the thrones
of thousands stand,
begins to turn,
and antique appetite for crowns
rolls menacingly
there behind my blood.
My shoulders feel a thirst
for purple,
but I fly.

ODE TO A HAWK

I watched the distant hawk above the trees
and marveled, as I always do,
to see the welcome of his self to wind,
his frailty against the blue,
the tautness of his wings before the sky,
the gleaming feathers in the sun;
the wholeness of his beauty in my world
left all the art of earth undone.

And as I watched the wonder of his grace,
a motion caught his seeking eye:
he circled, tilted, closed his wings,
and dropped—a comet from the sky.
He plummeted among the shadowed trees,
and there within the leafy dark,
in silent ways he found his prey
and stopped the gentle singing of a lark.

TO A MONK

I wonder, brother, if the world can know
what happens here within your wall, below
the silent cloistered arches of your love.

I wonder if they sense the cool
baptizing sanctity of peace you pour
upon their frantic, whirling, city wheels,
their mad metallic din, their motors' roar;

Or do they see the clear redemption here
of all their gaudy, baubled, spangled dress
within the mumbling wonder of the fair
and dim and antique splendor of your Mass?

And can they guess that in the solemn joy
of your be-altared and oft-officed days
there is a saving breath of second birth
for every bawdy eye and painted face?

Then, brother, raise your wall around their sin
and baptize all the blinded world within
the silent cloistered arches of your love.

'TWIXT DINNER AND THE TREE

The Beloved gathered those two years
about his youthful shoulders,
hunched against the ridicule
and cold
and stood
            beneath the Tree.

        Old wildly verbal Peter had already felt his words
        twist back, his promises stumbling to unanticipated oblivion;
        poor James hid dark in tears in some far kosher corner;
        the others, hidden here and there,
        secreted then midst worry and despair.
        The strong, the adequate, the certain, and the fled.

Only the boy absorbed the price of promise,
        evangel, news-bearer, the Beloved.

He did not understand the wind,
or time, or tide of magic
which had swept him to that table, to that breast, and hill
but only that incomprehensibly he loved
            beneath the Tree.

That name and heritage I claim, that John, that lover,
so in the fearful wonder of certain ceremony,
beneath the weight and mystery of word,
I speak with care what I have said to God before:
"You are why I have been."

Warmth at night,
your breast at supper, or
a lone Johannine place
beneath your Tree,

Or solitude.

That will be what I see among the hills and valleys of forever.

VERITAS INCARNATUS

Gentle, gentle from the flaming door;
gentle, from the sword-gilt gate;
fashioned in the dragon's antique roar;
begotten in the black bull's hate.

Risen through the white nomadic sands;
blazoned on the bright mercuric screen;
twisted under gypsies' oaken hands;
whispered by the dark world's queen.

Finished as it filled the musty cave,
blurted red the black and hallowed tree,
saved the dove, the lamb, the slave,
and came to Be.

WHAT ONE HAS DONE

I think it is less fun here
now
here in the garden plot—
although the moons still sail,
and suns still rise.

What one has done is push the I away from me,
is learn the magnet draws from elsewhere, not from here,
is see the who I was
against more quiet skies,
some russet autumn woods,
some stiller water.

I do know
there is still thunder:
I rolled and rumbled with it once,
and hurricanes I howled within an earlier sky,
the quakes I shook in lands and mountains.

But I know more about the peal, the blast, the wind, and tremor,
and I chose the twilight meadow
for my now.

YGDRASIL

Dark boughs that held the burden
That unheavened Adam and his brood,
And, leafless, bore the Christ,
The holy Body and the Blood,
    Bend now to me. Bring low thy boughs
    And turn thy leaves that I may see
    If thou wilt be within my life
    The source of joy or agony,
For I am wound and bound with thee,
And turn, as I will ever turn,
To seas and hills and stars and trees
For all the truth my heart can learn;
    And if you mean to bear me high
    And lift my bleeding limbs above,
    Then tell me now that I may know,
    And ready all my world for love,
Lest at the end I find that I
Have asked another one to give
Instead of pouring out my life,
My blood, on which a world may live.
    Am I to find within thy boughs
    The fruit of bread and wine for me?
    Or must I bleed, another Christ,
    And starve to loveless death on thee?

PROUDLY HE GOES

He brushed his hair and cocked his hat;
he drew the blinds and locked the door;
he walked the street and passed the shops.
The flower woman stepped aside;
the butcher shook his head;
the peddler ducked and cursed;
the policeman whistled, shook his fist;
the lamppost dodged away;
the streets stepped back;
the curbs kneeled down.
The shops to homes,
the signs to trees gave way,
the homes to fields.
the river
held his body for a moment,
then let it slowly down
and gently kept
his hat afloat.

LIGHT TODAY

Light today exploded below the grasses
and surprised me and meadows
with a kind of coming we remember—
an aria in yellow white.

We had settled for a lecherous peek
And a squeak of sentiment,
For the absence of amazement.

We had settled
                for impotence
until
light today.

TIME IS FLYING NOW

O Lady, will you walk with me
In some sweet-spangled meadow
And down along some hedgerowed lane
And through some lilied shadow?

O Lady, will you speak with me
By some fair willowed river
And say the words I never thought
To hear again forever?

O Lady, time is flying now
And my young breast is hollow
And when we two have walked and talked,
O, I'll be dead tomorrow.

LAMENT OF PAN (PETER)

Moon-skipping bovines are earth-bound
Felines again bare-footed;
Geese have forsaken maternity,
And beanstalks have been uprooted.

Toads have misplaced their autos,
Bears have forgotten balloons;
Rabbits no longer wear watches
And blackbirds remember no tunes.

Tigers don't melt as they used to,
Castles are gone from the sky;
Puppets are hopelessly wooden;
And we have forgotten to fly.

TO THE MATADOR

I burst to you;
I cried
the whole carousel
of a bright day to you.
I brought the breath of earth,
the crushed grass,
the straw of summer to you.
I carried all the fields upon my back,
beneath my feet
into the dusty circle of the city.
I brought you all I could of life.

And then they pierced,
they beat me.
I looked to you,
my gifts sweating away,
my eyes reddening.

Another stab
and the blindness of
your flash of red.
I followed through and through
and then your sword
I drank into my brain
and brought you
my soul.

And they cried
for you,
"Ole!"

CALVARY

O Calvary,
  how high,
  how once and blessed once
  you were.
Can you promise me
  that a daily hill
  is no higher than yours?

MY FATHER

It is nothing but
　　my father
　　standing at a window
　　looking down upon his
　　　dawn-haired son.
It is nothing but
　　his happiness
　　and the rising of his tears.
It is
　　nothing.

ESCAPE

He leaped
the floe-caked river
dancing,
seeming to,
in flight
skipping
in a deadly
hop-scotch.
Expediency
choreographed
his fear,
his foe
pirouetted him
in terror.
He balanced,
leaped,
and bled,
and, gasping, leaped again.

We noticed his
bleeding
dash
and clapped our hands
at the antics.

THE ETRUSCAN MASTER

Wait.
That was an error,
        that one,
        that bust that awes you,
I gave it to a child—
I gave it away
            to a child
            to play with.
The rest were better,
            greater
        but they were wrecked
        and burned.
Everything is gone now
        except that error
            and your silly awe.

WITHIN THE FLESH

Certainty conceives
    within the womb of act,
but the cycle moves
    to frame
    another newly-unknown face
    immediately
which grows perceptibly
    to surety
    within the flesh
    of the next
                doing.

PETER AND I

Do we always wake to cock-crow
from our bed
or from our dreamy treachery?
Waker or awaker
who cries loudly
or so much
within our world
enough
to pierce our wall
of other-hate?
What tongue can cock us back
to home
and make us know
the stony I,
the calcine soul,
and let us weep
to joy again a dawn
we should have known
would come?

Can no one
chanticleer at twilight
and spare us night?

OLD DUNBARTON CHURCH

She perched lightly
on the cobwebs of antiquity,
confidently aiming at today.
Anciently and patiently,
reverently, irrelevantly,
white peaked high
and elsewhere—
some old woman,
sure
that she still can.

And one passing
without asking,
never by the way noticing
missing all
away.

The smooth prayer of ninety years;
the dust of cornered, captured lusts,
willing and unwilling bonds,
and their stains
and scars of sought and unsought
births and washings,
nurtures and dyings.

Her own reality beholds itself.
She, justified and satisfied,
lies her own surprises.

SHIPWRIGHT

Her sails shook down, flapped, caught
the wind, snapped taut against
the spars, fought against the tug
in deep procession and a liturgy
of gathering grace to meet the swells.
She rose and trembled,
found the sea
and flew.

No gull or blowing whale will wonder
at her way, her wings, or care for line
or grace, or suck his breath to see her
come about against the wind, or long
to catch her ensign in a glass
as I.

This is her trial and mine.
If she learned all the love my fingers
taught, and all I brought of skill
and dream or sought of fame she will
ride storm and wind and calm until
in certainty and pride she will
before she dies,
sail home.

INCARNATUS

Bethlehem broadened and filled our horizons,
The stable demanded our hearts in return;
God spoke the Word in the flesh of a Man-child
And wrote with that Body what mankind must learn.

Suffer, he said, but never cause suffering;
Give, while the rest of the world seeks to take;
Die, if it's needed, but never cause dying;
Love, with the knowledge that friends may forsake.

Peace is your hope while others are warring;
Gentle, your way while the rest are all strong;
Care in a world that has grown past all caring;
Sing to a world that despises your song.

This is your duty, and this your commission:
To dance among those who creep on the earth;
To celebrate life amid deathly confusion,
To speak in your living the truth of my Birth.

ANTIQUES

The granite
of the old gods you saw,
remarked the chisel-work,
made note of line and shadow,
appreciated the jaw curve,
this fillet, that curl,

But never saw
the washing, welling light
behind the hollow eyes,
hoping for
empowering devotion.

You worship masks
and call them men,
and pass this deep life off
as artifact.

But they remember
and when he comes
who frees them from their stone,
they will attack your dreams
and send you
screaming in the night,
mask-lover.

EXPLORATION

Once we had a mystery
and a place to go,
reaches
and spaces,
faltered
and failing lines.
Once hopes engraved
(as wise men saw)
in possible
and scarce-labeled
fields of green and rose,
free from the oppression
of men's names,
Serendipity still a possibility,
an aspirant geography,
capable
beyond the failure
of the dubious bounds;
Seas were bridges then
and mountains stairs.

But that is gone
(as wise men said)
by consumption of the land
in the swallowings of men.
There are no more tomorrows
pregnant of capability,
no edges,
frames of vision,
dream acres struggling with horizons.

Only now
one arcane cavern
deep,
unsunned.
All hope can only turn now
down
to delve
internal landscapes
to drop from ledges of adventure
(as the wise men said)
sailing boiling seas
and making blind beachheads
beneath the silent cliffs

The desert left to die in
all lie there
and we must learn to hunt
and husband on their terms.
A golden city lies
(the wise men say)
among those sands,
But that is for tomorrow
And its mystery.

MY SOUL SO

Definition is the ultimate defense
    and if my shape is borrowed
    from validities next-door
    then I am infancy
    dandled on the knees out there.

Once I hanged a swing
        upon a long low bough
    but I could not treat my soul so.

My center must be low and close
    lest the chair tip
    when I reach for it,
            needing.

Then if there is failure
        or starvation
    it will all go when I do,
And it will be okay.

ME FATHER

Me father worked 'is brandied dander up
        on Sa'days
An beat hell outta me
        for me own good.
So I found out
        'bout God
Who I could fin'lly say,
        "Buzz off" to
        easier 'n me father.

A PROPHET SHOULD

Most of the time
a prophet is a distinct disadvantage,
knotting and burdening.
God-gripped oracles
make a body glum,
and all life limps in view of sibyls,
confining and confusing.

A prophet should resolve,
facilitate, ease, answer,
and console.

But shoulds are alien to him
and judgment echoes off his walls.

TO VIETNAM CASUALTY #50,472

If you died today
then
it might be your life
        that fled into mine.
It came from somewhere else,
bursting into my head
        as it must have screamed out of yours.

What can I do with such a quota?
Is there some new responsibility
        for me,
        for you?
Do I pay for you
        or have you paid for me
        debtlessly?

I did not choose it,
        rather would not have I,
but, certain that it could be wasted
        I accept the investment.
I will live twice deeply
        twice carefully now
                for you.

STIGMATA

ORIGINS

Don Quixote:

In an angel's momentary madness
(unable to withstand
or understand
his wrench of inactivity
against the wave of evil)
he touched me,
and cursed me with insanity
(if all the world is sane).
I do not brood,
but at my prayers I hope against
the cross of vision
and the foolishness of dream
and beg a silent beggar's death.

It may have been the moon
or an unlucky star
that paled the sweating forehead
of my mother
and stilled the grunts
that brought mc into being
before I cried a word,
before I had a way
to say a "no"
or know the cost
of "yes."

Or it may have been a dream she thought,
an herb she ate,
and I could feel it twist along the cord
that made me hers
and strike my bellied breast
until my soul was marked.
and I have borne it since.

A child,
I heard a song
among the hedge of lilacs,
and it scattered leaden soldiers
as the lilies watched
the shattering simplicity
of infancy unveiled
and darkened
by a mist of meaning.

And the boy breathed hard
beneath the heaviness
of a black tau
upon his forehead.

A dolphin mothered me;
a dragon
or a griffin
gave me suck,
and warped that simple manhood
into the world of wonder;
and I hunger
ever since
for the milk of dragons.

I was the one mistake of God:
he never meant me
for the earth.
I would have made a fine
Venusian child,
for I was built of dream
and all that world is dreams
instead of slag heaps
and the monster breath of death.

On the sands of earth
I writhe,
lost and burned
by ugliness.

I was conceived
within the sea
and walk the mountain
as a stranger
paces in an air
he finds remote within
the hunger of his lungs,
feeling the desert
as discovery and pain.

But from whatever womb
or wand,
I am
a singer in a dumb world
and a bird
among the deep-footed men.

There is a heaviness
to be.

Sancho Panza:

A stumble brought me into heaven
and I tripped my way
into salvation.
Never aiming at a star,
I ended walking
on its splendid plains.

I know the earth—
although I couldn't say to you
the words
about the way it feels
between my palms—
and leather
and its smells and strength,
and beasts
and all their ways:
I know the earth.

I saw the circle of my life:
I felt around its edges
and knew its endings.
I was aware of where it had to stop.

But he shattered neatness,
skimmed geometry into the sky
and wrenched my nerves.

That solid extension
in space and time
of a wife

and hearths
and roofs and stables,
supper and the child,
retreated,
beaten gray before
they even entered on the field.
Deeds and boundaries,
taxes and the tithe,
bushels, calves, and breakfast
scuttled off
beyond remembrance
and the stomach, bowels, and forehead
followed hard upon the heart.

Dream touched honesty
above the dung,
and sounds the soul remembers
from before the earth
sing songs
that reach below the flesh
and find their
revelation in what is a man.

But harps unstring
without him.

The rule of gray commands
except beneath his rusting shadow,
and that shade
turns suns
to shame.

I suppose
for you
I ought to call it love,
but even wordless I
can understand
how too pale that flies
against the skies of here and now.

I lost the "I" once-treasured
and became the dream-lord
who, if he could near disdain,
would look with it
upon the former world,
its breathing
and its summer silliness
that once was life.

But now I breathe
the newer air
and taste it in my throat
like honey
and the lotus.

Do I sleep?
Then dreams I praise,
and dreams I find
the only reason for
    a woman's pangs of birth,
and I cry you, "Dream!"

Aldonza:

To reach back and down
for roots
is hollow as theology.
I spring more deeply
than man or woman thinks,
and find my tap root
sucks its being
from the Styx:
Charon great-grandfathered me
before the hordes
of others.

I was umothered,
so do I unmother me,
and, remembering no birth,
I will not bear.
No man-child will come out of me
as men too often enter.
None of myself will I give
to a world
that hated me enough
to make me be.

I will be party
to the feel and the condition
my twisted genes assigned.
This heritage I never knew
could carry with the blood,
but here I am:
of a clod, a clod;

of a flesh, a flesh,
of the body of a whore, a whore—
and a good one—
the best beneath the queen.

I come from the soil,
from the people
and the mud.
You all made me,
as you made the witch last spring,
and you will burn me, too,
when you can't stand
to be without me anymore,
when you have worked your own enchantment
and need to destroy your sins.

The end of me
will be a genesis,
but the constant "Why?"
will epitaph my dust
until you all are dead
who live my death.

I am from you—
and bless you with a curse
from here
within my daily grave.

A C T S

Don Quixote:

Do they think
behind the smug pink blindness
of their cheeks
I do not know?
Do they think I have eyes
that do not see the rust,
the horse's boney sides, the windmill?

There is no glory in the gold
unless it gilds the sand
and stands like light
in virtue
only as it turns
the dross of darkness
from its deep descending path
or uses clay
to heal a blind man's eyes.

The action of a mind
baptizes
and realizes
the breath beneath the grass.

The world I take as paint and clay.
I turn it inside out
to find a place to be
and march
until each tree has freed its elf,
each rock its gnome,
and all is true.

I hold the earth
between the love of sky and water,
and the emptiness of night
finds reason for the love.

I bless the child, the bush, the bird,
and free the light,
and start again
the waves
beneath the hills
that lamb about my horse's feet.

I know ashes from stardust,
but feel the reason in my years
must bring them near
and let them see
the threads of nature that they share.
I wear them both
with equal grace
and love.

I found a touch
would open all the hungry doors
of plains and mountains,
dozing in their three days' sleep
behind the stone:
they thirst for me,
my sword, my song.
They rested till I came
and knew that I would come.

I cry the joy aloud
to see becoming here on every hand,
and weep before the blindness
of my race
which saved the world for poetry
but bound itself,
as I am bound
to mourn its death.
Men do not know and do not want
the sprite that raises breasts
and roars beneath the blood.
They settle them for wives
and firesides and whores
when they are bored.

I can redeem
the tree, the sea,
the horn, the shell,
the dog,
but not the man.

This is the heaviness to bear
behind my shield.

Sancho Panza:

We pots
find conversation
with the potter difficult,
interrogation quite beyond belief,
but we clay our way
to happiness and reason
by donation.

You laugh at me
because I ride the ass
beside his horse
and leap at his whisper,
and kiss his hand.

I did not flee,
you'll notice,
when you jeered:
I bent my head,
and ran to hold his stirrup.

Won't you wonder why?

Could I so join his mission
if I see you wonder?
Could you think there might
be depths of causes
you have missed?
And find a way to ask
about a love?

We clods carry souls
and sometimes,
spared the shrouds
of delicate theology
the minded wear,
we can come nearer God.

You laugh because
you think it must be understood
and you don't understand
there is no stronger impetus

for earth than mystery.
And, never thinking,
I find the deepest reasons
for my mother's pangs of birth.

One walks
into a deeper truth
by finding and facing
the balance match
between myself and him.

If I have lost myself,
I were well lost,
and the world richer,
and the green deeper,
and the sun above the hill.

I stumble now
(and always have)
and you may laugh,
but now I limp
towards light.

Aldonza:

A preacher beds the best!
That neat conjunction—
  piety and passion—
  is the only twist of novelty
  I know
  (the only time
  I think a little
  of the fun).

And so I tingle just a bit
and wait to see
his armor dropped aside
and hear his battle songs
reduce to hums
within my ear.

I wonder—
will he best the padre?

CONCLUSIONS

Don Quixote:

Good night!
Lay the sword somewhere
against his birth tomorrow.
I tell you clear there is another.
Once I met him,
once we rode and sang
across the high north country.
They tell me that he sleeps
within some cavern
of the earth,
but he will hear my death
and ride.

The sword is his.

Tell him to weep.

That is the way.

Sancho Panza:

I am a footprint,
an epitaph,
and never in the world
will one decide
to honor me.

I am a letter sealed
and world and world
will look
and pass it on.

But one will know
the wordless, soundless song
and match the harmony
from where he is.
And since he hears,
I sing.

Aldonza:

But you were cruel
to take the only death
I have to die
and steal it from the world
and me
to be your own
forever.

AVE MARIA

ANNUNCIATION

Canto I

I tried to look,
but there was too much light,
and I could only bend and fall,
disabled,
unfit to speak
the kind of ritual this royal visitor
had rights to—
this passing wonder,
this courier of glory.

"But…how can it be?"
The poor, pathetic, dull, unlettered me,
a fool unused to ceremony,
daring only my common practicality
in the very face
of a starry son of bliss.

The willing condescension of this perfect one,
himself a paraphrase of the celestial ideal,
essayed for me
a simplification of Simplicity himself,
to let me know
I could not know,
but with my "Yes,"
it could be so.

Then, as he left, the bright one,
what was it?
Something—
like a whisper left behind?
a sigh?
I don't know:
a touch of fragile wing?
A fluttered breath of vague and early summer?
A word, was it?
A shadow?
I don't remember.
How could I know?

Or was it nothing?

Or only a tiny dot of hidden difference now,
some covert nub of novelty,
of intimate unfamiliarity
inside my breast?

Or is it only me?
Or only more of me?
Or even more than me?

And now…

This body never bore before;
it doesn't know the way.
Will someone?
Will waiting serve the full, bright meaning?

Am I to turn some corner now?
Become what I have never been?

Be new, somehow,
or strange?
Is there some pattern I should change,
some different way of walking through the day
which should be mine?

But I know no other.

What else is there to do?
To work, to rest,
to eat, to dream,
to wear my poor mind thin
trying in futility to understand.

So I must wait and wonder, then,
skipping back and forth from fear
to sweet anticipation,
dreading lest I dream too much
or want too much
beyond what has been given.

Canto II

And now I watch my gentle husband's eyes across the table,
wondering if
that dream he had
was strong enough for him?
Or 'round its edges
are there fringes, still, of hurt,
some lingered boundaries of mute forbearance,
in his bowed benevolence?

A woman wants to bear messiah
every time, every time,
but men,

what do they want?
Or do they have another kind of fear,
of other pangs we do not know?
A fear, perhaps, to be un-made
by him each woman wants?

My man, of all the men,
no other one could bear the muddled stew
of hope and grudging sorrow
I have given you.

They told me I would never love
an old man,
or have to sacrifice my joy
to please him.

They simply did not know
that giving would be
all gift for me.

MAGNIFICAT

Canto III

Elizabeth,
old mother, cousin, aunt,
my only one,
freshened with your own expectation,
similar, and stretched, like mine,
beyond the prospect of the ordinary,
you told me what I needed—
more than needed now—
to know,
And I am shattered and amazed
and not equipped;

willed and willing,
I am unprepared.

So I must only laud my Lord,
and sing and praise him,
for knowing what I do not even know,
for choosing me
and blessing me,
(and not the queen).

For Order himself
has reordered this world,
and turned away from all—
the pride, the strength, the wealth—
and gathered to himself
the weak, the hungry, and the poor
and me.

And so
one seems to hear
the echo of old words again,
old fragments from what they say
is men's talk at the synagogue,
old promises and antique covenants
that have grown faint and cold
in memory's weak hands.
And words float up:
"Wonderful," they say,
and
"Counselor," they say,
and
"Prince of Peace"?

But, this must stop!

I do not know;
I do not understand;
all I must do is wait
and drown the wild imaginings
inside a trusting silence,
till he comes.

All I must do is wait.

NATIVITY

Canto IV

We thought at first that I should stay at home,
while he went off to see to taxes and the census
but there was none to call on here,
so quieting his fears
I thought that I would go
—not knowing day or hour.

Oh, is it fair enough,
the hay I gathered here?
It is the unstitched bedding
of no caring grandam
but the Father by himself.
No choice of mine, no choice of ours,
But choice by him.

The cave, unbuilt by man,
but made by him.
For the child,

unmade by man
but made by him.

My man is in the village,
searching in this late last-minute
for a mid-wife of the town,
one to do
what he would fear to try
(the birth blood
would bar him from the temple
in clammy uncleanness, anyway).

I am ready.
Underdress is torn
to make the bands.
I know of nothing else to do.
There's water here
and warmth.
It has to be enough.

Now I know
the pains of Eve,
and now the baby comes.

SHEPHERDS

Canto V

The midwife's come and gone,
and how I want to sleep,
but there are others now,
as if conducted here
by pipe and drum and panoply.

They speak, instead, of stars and skies
and angels wondering,
so they say.

They, too, saw angels, then—
Heard them sing and bid them come?
What immense business must this be
which companies itself
with all the folk of heaven!

He lies, uncomprehending,
Center of it all,
smiling as he weaves experiments
with each small hand and foot,
turning dark and brand-new eyes
upon our silly donkey's tethered patience
in the near corner of the cave.

He slid into my world in silence,
eyes unnaturally wide,
and sucked the blood-milk
from my breast
before a dozen breaths.

After Gabriel, this one took me,
subdued my body
and all my soul,
but only now he draws the rest of me
into himself,
the rest of me,
the part I can see,
the part I willingly will be.

I think he does not know
his breakfast milk
flows from a breast that he devised,
a pattern born as he was born
forever in the Father's mind.

MAGI

Canto VI

I never heard before
the sounds of palaces,
the rustlings of silk on silk,
nor smelt the spicy musk
of cinnamon and cloves
about a man,
nor caught the liquid sputter
of old Persian talk.

How old they are and wise;
how sure they are and bold;
how far they came;
how weighty are their gifts.

Was Father Solomon
perhaps like this?
Enwrapped in wisdom and in balm,
and seeming kingly in his very step.

And I despair
within our simple house,
of offering
a proper hospitality,

a Jew's warm welcome
to the stranger/guest.

Are they surprised by us,
I wonder,
as we were awed by them?
When they sought a king
to find no palace and
no eunuchs and
no royal robes?
Is their awkward homage
and their clumsy deference
no more than foreignhood,
or did we disappoint them,
falling short in show
of what their star foretold?

But in their dark and Eastern eyes
I see no judgment or reproach—
only a kind of bafflement
which lightly veils a willing assent
to what,
to whom
their gods and stars have led them.

With no option now,
no way to back away,
they tentatively bow
and hesitantly here let lie
their gold, their incense,
and their myrrh,
useless elsewhere now,

intended still for royalty,
but royalty they cannot see.

Still confused,
confounded by the inexplicable,
they awkwardly depart
and go, quietly bearing
both the tincture of doubt
and teasing hint of possibility
that stars were not untrue.

Will the day come
when I should tell him
of his visitors,
these three wise old wandering Gentiles,
or spare him
such temptation to arrogance?

PURIFICATION

Canto VII

It is the blood,
the wise have said,
which sears and soils
and even sucks the power
out of prayer.

So, since I bled him into being,
I am polluted now
and I have spent
my forty days alone
(so I would taint no other

who, ignorant of this pollution,
might be soiled and spoiled
for prayer.)

But the white blood
of my breast
has been no soil, but life
for him.

Now if I want to keep my son,
now I must come
and buy him from the priests
and God,
for they have owned him
since his birth;
he has been theirs.
And I owe them now
if I would have him back.

Two pigeons
in trade
for the maker of birds.

FLIGHT TO EGYPT

Canto VIII

"No time to pack,"
my ancient dreaming man announced,
"We leave tonight."

I wanted not to go
and have a few more days,
but wanted safety more for him.

The donkey sighed his resignation:
Bethlehem at first, then Nazareth,
now somewhere we have never known.

Carpenters could work no matter where
but how to raise a boy,
a proper boy,
without the Temple?

Well, by the time he's seven
he may apprentice to some artisan,
to a potter mixing mud,
or to a tanner or a dyer.

I would rather all this fuss and do
with goyim were forgot,
were just forgot
until we can go home.

FINDING IN TEMPLE

Canto IX

How sure I am
it will not be remembered
as it really was:
the unintended selfishness
of the child-man,
that plain, unkind, uncaring
thoughtlessness,
the self-absorption
of a youth.

"I thought you would know…"
Not so! Not so!
He simply did not think at all!
He sat and wallowed in those arguments,
those old rabbinic challenges and queries:
"What does it mean?"
"What lies behind the syllables?"
"How can we tell a tale
to fill the void between those words?"
"What must have happened here
where Torah is so silent?"

And I saw them nodding,
generously and tolerantly listening
to his simple, budding penetrations
of the mysteries,
sometimes surprised at him.

I even listened
for a moment,
and smiled inside
(because that kind of thought in women
must be stilled).

"Enough of this!"
Strong hand on young wrist.
Joseph feeling the added bite of
"…my father's business,"
flung again into remembering
his fostering,
not fathering.
"We've wasted three whole days!"

I think the boy knew then;
I think he thought about it then
and knew
he had been wrong.
Submission was his apology,
just as afterward t'would be his glory.

BAPTISM

Canto X

What can a widowed mother do?
God gives a son only to tease?
That other something there
has taken him away from me.

His place is set at table here, but usually unfilled.
His bed is made, but always now unused.
His name is called, but commonly unanswered.

He has finally gone
from us.

The neighbor women told me.
they had seen him there
with wild, mad, camel-vested John;
and, oh, I know he goes to certain trouble
in those Jordan waters.

And then those stories
about a bird,
about a sound some called a voice!

It is too much
when piled upon my heap of misery,
my store of mystery.

How can it ever lead to good
when I,
when we
are left behind?

CANA WEDDING

Canto XI

It was even awkward,
somehow out of place,
to be there.
How could I share that day
with my strange, absent son…
and his odd friends?

I always try to twist reality,
to make apology
to family friends and other sons;
I strain out this excuse or that,
to shield them and myself
from oddity,
the inexplicable.

I hear the whispers:
"Mad," "Insane," "Beside himself"
and my widowed heart
so tempted then to nod,
disposed itself almost against all hope.

But in that dimness of doubt
I still remember angels,
and the shuffling shepherds' feet,
the rustling of alien silks,
and I know
it is the sheer obscurity
of sanctity…

So I stretch and say,
"Tell him the wine is gone."
and then the slap-down
"Madame, no!
Not yet!"

So there is a disappointment,
a small despair for me,
of unhope that he will ever mother-me
again—
although he acts reluctantly
and in the end…
well, he makes the wine.

ON THE WAY OF TEARS

Canto XII

Aie!
This is the end.
This is the fruit of
all these years?
This is what it comes to?

Oh, God,
what can you expect

from me?
How much can you ask?
Have you no heart?

This bloody, stumbling tangle of a man,
this knotted snag of flesh
beneath that heavy wood
is all that is left
of those high-flying words,
and fancy, airy wonders.
All that is left
of a son.

Oh!
See, he turns.
He twists his tattered sack of pulp
and squinting through
the spate of blood
beneath the thorns
he looks up
at me.
His eyes!

Agh! Agh!
I can only cry
and tear my veil.
I weep and weep,
and still I do not know
what it is
or why.

He left us long ago
and they all followed him

(where are they now?).
He was someone,
a stranger to his mother
until just now.

He could do all,
but can do nothing now
except to stumble on
and I, to wait
and watch.

CALVARY

Canto XIII

Sometimes, I know,
they die for days and days—
pinned naked,
hammered open,
unspared the sun and rain,
unshielded
from the vehemence,
the sniggering righteousness.
and smirking virtue
of the Pharisee.

So thin now,
here,
so still.

He is thirsting.
Here!
A stick!

Here—give him wine,
Oh, give him wine at last.

And let him go:
there is nothing more.

God, let him go, now.
Let him go.

Ah,
his last,
his whispered,
"Teshelam."

and then
a beaten, broken, battered peace
and silence,
and the gut-tremble of the earth—
the mountains knew—
the trees knew—
and the winds.

Since Bethlehem I wondered:
would I ever be old enough,
ever wise enough,
to fathom it.

But I have only stood
outside of everything
and seen
without knowing.

There was something
there...but...

NOTES

The Apple Tree

Heracles was the bastard son of Zeus and the greatest hero of Greek mythology. As punishment for a crime, he was forced to undertake twelve labors, one of which was to steal the golden apples of the Hesperides nymphs that were guarded by the dragon Ladon.

The Grail

Some of the legends of King Arthur and the Holy Grail consider the Grail to be the cup Jesus used at the Last Supper or the chalice of the Mass. *Offerimus* is the prayer said in the Latin Mass when the chalice is offered to God.

'Twixt Dinner and the Tree

John the Apostle was called "the disciple whom Jesus loved" in the Gospel. He was described as "lying on Jesus's breast" at the Last Supper and as being the only apostle who remained with Jesus during the crucifixion. Because legend has him still alive in the year 100 AD, he was considered to be little more than a teenager during Jesus's lifetime. I was named for him.

Ygdrasil

Ygdrasil is the name of the massive Tree of Life at the center of Norse mythology. The poem treats it as a counterpart to the Cross of Christ.

Stigmata

The fictional Don Quixote was a foolish dreamer who thought himself a proper knight. The earthy, illiterate Sancho Panza became his squire, and, in one tradition, Aldonza was a prostitute Quixote mistook for the Lady Dulcinea.

INDEX OF TITLES AND FIRST LINES

NOTE ABOUT THE AUTHOR

John Julian is a contemplative monk, priest, and scholar, and the founder of the monastic Order of Julian of Norwich in Wisconsin. Prior to monastic life, he served parishes in Wisconsin, New Hampshire, and Connecticut, taught at the University of Rhode Island and Hampshire College, and served as the Director of the Social Service Institute. As Father John Julian, OJN, he has published nine books in the field of scholarly religion, including *The Complete Julian of Norwich*, *The Complete Imitation of Christ*, and *The Complete Introduction to the Devout Life* which was recently named one of "The Top 100 Christian Books of All Time" by the *Church Times* in England. John Julian published poems in magazines and literary journals for a brief time fort-five years ago; since then, he has been writing in solitude. This is his first book of poetry.

ACKNOWLEDGMENTS

"Lament" was first published in *Poems Out Of Wisconsin*, 1961.

"Meeting" was first published in *Commonweal* magazine, 4/24/59.

"Veritas incarnatus" was first published in *Spiritus: A Journal of Christian Spirituality*, Spring 2015.

All other poems appear in print here for the first time.

ABOUT PARACLETE PRESS

Who We Are

Paraclete Press is a publisher of books, recordings, and DVDs on Christian spirituality. Our publishing represents a full expression of Christian belief and practice—from Catholic to Evangelical, from Protestant to Orthodox.

We are the publishing arm of the Community of Jesus, an ecumenical monastic community in the Benedictine tradition. As such, we are uniquely positioned in the marketplace without connection to a large corporation and with informal relationships to many branches and denominations of faith.

What We Are Doing

PARACLETE PRESS BOOKS Paraclete publishes books that show the richness and depth of what it means to be Christian. Although Benedictine spirituality is at the heart of all that we do, we publish books that reflect the Christian experience across many cultures, time periods, and houses of worship. We publish books that nourish the vibrant life of the church and its people—books about spiritual practice, formation, history, ideas, and customs.

We have several different series, including the best-selling Paraclete Essentials and Paraclete Giants series of classic texts in contemporary English; Voices from the Monastery—men and women monastics writing about living a spiritual life today; award-winning poetry; best-selling gift books for children on the occasions of baptism and first communion; and the Active Prayer Series that brings creativity and liveliness to any life of prayer.

MOUNT TABOR BOOKS Paraclete's Mount Tabor Books series focuses on liturgical worship, art and art history, ecumenism, and the first millennium church.

PARACLETE RECORDINGS From Gregorian chant to contemporary American choral works, our music recordings celebrate sacred choral music through the centuries. Paraclete Recordings is the record label of the internationally acclaimed choir Gloriæ Dei Cantores, praised for their "rapt and fathomless spiritual intensity" by *American Record Guide*, and the Gloriæ Dei Cantores Schola, which specializes in the study and performance of Gregorian chant. Paraclete Press is also the exclusive North American distributor of the recordings of the Monastic Choir of St. Peter's Abbey in Solesmes, France, long considered to be a leading authority on Gregorian chant.

PARACLETE VIDEO PRODUCTIONS Our DVDs offer spiritual help, healing, and biblical guidance for life issues: grief and loss, marriage, forgiveness, anger management, facing death, and spiritual formation.

Learn more about us at our website
www.paracletepress.com or phone us toll-free at 1.800.451.5006

SCAN
TO
READ
MORE